JOSEF MENGELE

JOSEF MENGELE

JEREMY KLAR AND
HENRIETTA M. LILY

Published in 2016 by The Rosen Publishing Group, Inc.
29 East 21st Street, New York, NY 10010

Copyright © 2016 by The Rosen Publishing Group, Inc.

First Edition

Library of Congress Cataloging-in-Publication Data

Klar, Jeremy, author.
Josef Mengele / Jeremy Klar and Henrietta M. Lily. — First Edition.
    pages cm — (The Holocaust)
Includes index.
ISBN 978-1-5081-7047-1 (library bound)
1. Mengele, Josef, 1911–1979—Juvenile literature. 2. War criminals—Germany—Biography—Juvenile literature. 3. World War, 1939–1945—Atrocities—Juvenile literature. 4. Germany—Social conditions—1933–1945—Juvenile literature. 5. Physicians—Germany—Biography—Juvenile literature. I. Lily, Henrietta M., author. II. Title.
DD247.M46K53 2016
940.53'18092—dc23
[B]

2015014581

Manufactured in China

CONTENTS

INTRODUCTION

They arrived by the thousands: Jews, Catholics, Gypsies, and Jehovah's Witnesses; prisoners of war from the Soviet Union and Poland; and the physically and mentally challenged. After spending days on a train—not a passenger train but a cattle car meant for livestock—they arrived. They didn't come to this place for vacation, school, or work. They were brought here against their will, to be murdered.

Before the exhausting journey, many of the Jews had struggled to survive in the ghettos. All of their belongings were taken from them, but they remembered how, months prior, they had been in school, run businesses, or played outdoor games with friends and family. They had lived normal lives. All of them had names, but in the camps, these, too, were taken from them. In place of their birth names, they were given numbers, which were tattooed onto their arms. Along with the numbers came the harsh reality that they now belonged to Germany and its Third Reich.

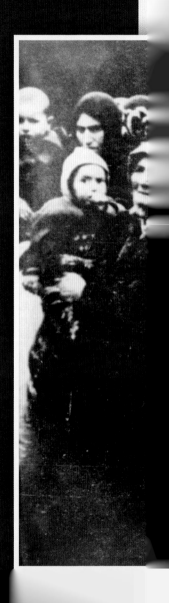

Hungarian Jews arrive in large numbers to one of Nazi Germany's most notorious concentration camps, Auschwitz, in the summer of 1944. Newly arrived prisoners would file into the camp where they would immediately be sorted in a process known as selection. Some were sent to do labor, while others were sent—unknowingly—straight to their deaths.

If you had been with them in this cattle car, you would have seen how their last days were spent. They were crammed into the trains without food or drink. In order to relieve themselves, they had to use a single bucket. Some trains didn't have buckets—or even blankets—just the hard floor beneath. Many people died on the trains. On several trips, the bodies were not removed until the train reached its final destination. Imagine being herded into a cramped, filthy space. Imagine that next to you is the body of a loved one who has just died. It's a horrifying thought, but it was reality for millions of innocent prisoners—mostly Jews—during World War II.

This true story of torture doesn't end with the train trip. When the train met its destination, German soldiers were waiting outside with guns. They ordered the prisoners out with aggressive shouting. The prisoners were tired, starving, and confused. Some of the prisoners already knew of this place—they had received postcards from relatives who had been sent here. Little did they know that the postcards had been falsely written, and that their relatives were most likely dead. Little did they know that they had been brought to the Third Reich's largest death camp, Auschwitz.

The German soldiers roughly guided hundreds of prisoners out onto the railway platform. Whatever valuables the prisoners had been allowed to bring were now hurriedly left behind. The prisoners were instructed to form two lines, one for men and one for women. They were about to undergo one of the most haunting ordeals of the Holocaust— the *Selektionen*. This was the process by which the Nazis—headed by Nazi doctors—decided who would become slaves in the labor camp and who would be murdered immediately.

Prisoners were instructed by a *Selektionen*, or selection, doctor to go either to the right or left. Going to the right meant that they would join the labor camp where they would be worked to death. Going to the left meant that this would be their last day on Earth. Those sent to their deaths were deemed unfit for slave work. Most children, elderly, disabled people, and pregnant women were immediately sent to die. Those sent to the left did not know that they would soon be dead. They were led to believe that they needed to take showers before entering the labor camp.

They were marched in long lines to the shower buildings. Electrified fences surrounded the walkway to the showers. Some prisoners, sensing doom, threw themselves on the fences and committed suicide. Once in the locked shower unit, a toxic gas was released and the prisoners painfully choked to death on the fumes. More than one hundred prisoners were murdered during each gassing. These mass murders took place several times a day.

The prisoners who survived Auschwitz remember a German soldier and doctor who took an uncanny pleasure in leading the selection process. His name was Dr. Josef Mengele, and he was known as the Angel of Death. His personality was a combination of pleasantness and perversity. He stood on the railway platform in an impeccable uniform with white gloves. He often had a cheerful expression on his face and was heard humming classical music by many prisoners. He wore perfectly polished boots and held a riding crop. Many times his pleasant demeanor would turn wicked, and he would beat prisoners with his crop while shouting at them. He would often send otherwise healthy prisoners to their deaths because they had skin blemishes or minor imperfections.

Mengele's eyes would widen in excitement whenever he encountered twins at the selections process. He, like many other Nazi doctors, used the prisoners for experimentation. He was especially interested in twins. Nazi doctors knew that the prisoners were going to die anyway, so prisoners were used for numerous deadly experiments. Most of the experiments were of little or no value to medical science, and most were cruel and barbaric. These men called themselves doctors, but instead of healing the sick, they caused the suffering, disease, torture, and deaths of millions of innocent human beings.

CHAPTER ONE

MENGELE'S YOUTH

O f the notorious villains who participated in the tragic events of the Holocaust, the infamous Nazi doctor Josef Mengele particularly stands out. Mengele was a man of emotional and mental extremes. He was highly intelligent, a doctor of known academic intelligence, and yet he was able to take pleasure in a senseless process that brought millions of victims to their deaths. He was cruel toward the majority of the Jews and other prisoners who were brought to Auschwitz, but gentler toward the hundreds of twins and other prisoners that he used as research subjects for his personal interests. Many of the twins and Gypsy children of the camp even referred to him as "Uncle Pepi." His gentleness could end abruptly, though. He personally led some of the children to their deaths in the gas chambers.

Many Auschwitz survivors witnessed and remember his contradictions. He was a cultivated, good-looking man, yet during a moment of anger he could become a savage. This man of contradictions was more than a doctor gone wrong. He was part of a whole system that had

Dated 1938, this photograph shows Josef Mengele early in his career as a doctor for the Nazi party. Even within Nazi Germany, few could ever fathom the extreme experiments that Mengele would carry out during his time at Auschwitz.

gone wrong. He was a man following a demented system of beliefs that were deeply rooted in his upbringing. These beliefs were supported by many parts of German society and government. As a youth, he was exposed to these corrupt beliefs. He would later use them to justify his own actions as a murderous doctor.

Josef Mengele's beliefs allowed him to use humans as guinea pigs and to send many people to their deaths without feeling remorse or shame. His beliefs allowed him to behave more like a monster than a doctor. He never faltered in his wrongheaded belief that he and the Nazi organization were doing what was right for the German people. To him, the crimes and injustices that the Nazis committed were necessary for the welfare of Germany and, ultimately, for the good of Europe as a whole.

GERMANY BEFORE WORLD WAR II

Josef Mengele was born in Germany on March 16, 1911—three years before World War I. The war took place mostly in Europe and involved many of the world's most powerful countries. The events that took place before and after World War I played a major role in shaping the lives of many Germans, including Mengele. Many historians believe that one of the causes of the war was that each country involved had its own strong sense of nationalism.

Nationalism is a political philosophy or belief that the welfare of one's nation is the most important thing. In this definition, the word "nation" means any community or culture with its own territory and government. The sense of nationalism in a country is strengthened if the people of that country share common characteristics. These characteristics can include ethnic background, religion, language, history, and moral beliefs.

Each country can have its own idea of what is best for its welfare. A country's nationalist beliefs are established and enforced on many levels. Adults and rulers establish nationalist beliefs through a government or ruling unit. Children and teens are taught nationalist beliefs in school, church, youth groups, their family, and through the media. Josef Mengele was born at a time when Germany's sense of nationalism was very strong. The German Empire promoted the belief that Germany could be the preeminent power in Europe—and even the world. This belief led Germany into World War I.

Austria-Hungary started the war on July 28, 1914, motivated by nationalist concerns. Germany decided to support Austria-Hungary in the war. In a military maneuver on August 2, 1914, Germany sought to attack France by way of Belgium. Belgium was neutral—that is, it took no active part in the war—and would not permit German troops to travel across its territory. Not willing to back down, Germany decided to cross Belgium by force. The

On November 11, 1918, a late night special edition of the *Evening Standard* announces the end of World War I, then known as the Great War. Many of the terms of the treaty that brought peace after World War I punished Germany and fueled national resentment.

following day, Great Britain declared war on Germany for its act against Belgium.

The war lasted longer than anyone could have imagined, and it devastated many areas of Europe. On October 4, 1918, after four years of massive destruction and countless lost lives, Germany asked for terms of a truce. Because of changes that arose from the war, the empires of Europe were overthrown and replaced by new governments. The German Empire, led by the Kaiser, was replaced with a new German government called the Weimar Republic. In answer to Germany's request for

In the period following World War I, economic restrictions placed on Germany caused a major depression, including shortages in housing. In this photograph, taken in Berlin in July 1920, a family is shown living in an old train car.

a truce, the Allies created the Treaty of Versailles. The treaty demanded that Germany accept full responsibility for the war. It also placed many restrictions on Germany.

During the following years, Germany faced a deep economic depression. Many Germans blamed the loss of the war and the resulting financial depression on the liberal leaders of the Weimar Republic. Many of those liberal leaders were Jewish. Soon, many Nationalist Germans were saying that the liberal Jews had tricked Germany into accepting the treaty in order to weaken the German state. Some Germans also suggested that the terms of the Treaty of Versailles must be broken. Many Germans believed that, whatever the cost, Germany had to once again become an empire.

TREATY OF VERSAILLES

The Treaty of Versailles was the peace treaty that ended World War I between Germany and the Allied Powers. The Allied Powers primarily consisted of the United States, the British Empire, France, Italy, and Japan. Determined to prevent such hostility from reoccurring on the European continent, the Allies used the treaty to force Germany to let go of territories, colonies, and large military groups. Germany lost 25,000 square miles of territory, which contained about 7 million people. Much of the land Germany ceded became independent states or was annexed to bordering nations. Much of the lost territory was rich in resources and had German-speaking residents.

Germany furthermore faced major restrictions on the size of its armed forces. The German army was shrunk to a maximum size of 100,000 men. Only three military schools were allowed to persist for training. Civilian staff and the police force were reduced in size, and paramilitary forces were forbidden. While these terms may sound harsh enough, the reparations that the Treaty of Versailles demanded were far harsher on Germany.

As part of Article 231, commonly called the "War Guilt Clause," Germany was required to make payments for war damages in excess of 132 billion gold Marks, or about 31.4 billion dollars. Germany also had to explicitly accept blame for World War I and the destruction that ensued. As severe as the terms of the Treaty of Versailles were, the leaders of Germany's newly founded Weimar Republic saw no alternative and accepted the treaty's conditions. This acceptance humiliated many nationalist Germans, who felt that Germany was superior and had been cheated of victory.

THE RISE OF ANTI-SEMITISM AND DARWINISM

The Germany in which Josef Mengele grew up placed heavy emphasis on nationalism, hatred of Jews, and the importance of German superiority. Hatred of Jews, or anti-Semitism, has occurred for thousands of years throughout the world. This hatred stems from differences in religious and cultural beliefs. Anti-Semitism is spread largely through literature. Literary works can influence any nation's interests, beliefs, and philosophies.

Several anti-Semitic works were written before and during the time of Mengele's youth, World War I, and the German depression. German anti-Semitic works were written by respected doctors, professors, politicians, and even religious leaders such as Martin Luther. Luther founded the Lutheran church and spoke against the Jews because they would not accept Jesus as their savior.

The German hatred of Jews was also politically driven. Many Germans believed that because Jews adhered to their own set of rules and customs, they were a threat to a structured German society. Because of Jewish religious practices, Jewish people seemed different from non-Jewish Germans. Non-Jewish Germans felt especially threatened by the fact that German Jews were finding their way into prominent and powerful positions in German society.

Widespread paranoia led to rumors about Jewish plots to take over the world. Seeking to heighten this paranoia, some highly influential anti-Semitic books were published and sold in vast numbers. The books helped to establish the acceptance of strong anti-Semitism throughout Germany. Anti-Semitic political works were being written as early as 1905, six years before Mengele was born and more than ten years before the German depression. Just thirty years later, Germany would turn into a country that practiced anti-Semitism on a large and murderous scale.

During the time of Josef Mengele's youth, there was also a strong emphasis on evolutionary philosophies, one in particular being Darwinism. Darwin's theory of evolution states that species that are more fit or adapted to their environment will survive, whereas those species that are less fit or adapted to their environment will perish. Some scientists began to apply the principles of Darwinism to human beings. This is called Social Darwinism. Beginning in the late 1800s, groups of scientists researched ways to improve the genetic quality of the human species. This research was part of a set of beliefs called eugenics.

Eugenic scientists believed that the careful breeding of humans would lead to a stronger, more perfect human species. Scientists looked for ways of breeding stronger humans and avoiding weaker offspring. It was believed that people with physical and mental disabilities made the human species weaker. Soon, in many parts of the world (including the United States), the sterilization of physically and mentally challenged people became common-place. When a person is sterilized, he or she can no longer have children. It was thought that by sterilizing those with disabilities, all weaknesses in humans could be eliminated.

Several important Germans took the tenets of eugenics and applied them to Germany on a nationalist level. They believed that Germany should have an empire again, and that the German people were genetically superior. They wanted to separate Germans from the rest of the human species. In addition, many Germans believed that non-Germans—and Jews, in particular—were weak. Jewish people were no longer thought of as religiously different but also as racially different.

Political cartoons and propaganda reinforced stereotypes about the differences between Aryan Germans and Jews. This 1935 illustration depicts the Aryan German worker as fit, blond, and healthy. The Jew, in contrast, is shown as an overweight, balding profiteer.

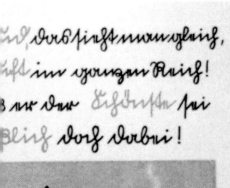

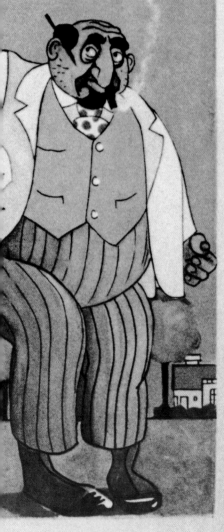

In the late 1800s, German books and articles were published that outlined a battle of survival between Jews and Aryans. The German definition of Aryan was a person from northern Europe having blond hair and blue eyes. The idea that the German, or Aryan, race was locked in battle with other races for survival would become the main preoccupation of the Nazi movement in years to come.

JOSEF'S YOUTH

Being raised in the wake of World War I was difficult for most of the German population. Many middle-class households went without food and money. Josef Mengele was raised in a less burdened household because his family was upper class. His family did not suffer during the depression as others did—in fact, his family profited in the years following World War I.

Josef was born to Karl and Walburga Mengele. He was the eldest of three sons. The family lived in Günzburg, which is a small picturesque German town located on the banks of the Danube River. His parents owned a foundry that made farming equipment. When Josef was born, Karl already had more than ten people working for the company.

Josef's parents felt a strong sense of German nationalism. When World War I started in 1914, Karl left to serve in the war. During this time, Walburga ran the foundry business. She was a fierce and talented businesswoman. She established a manufacturing contract with the German Kaiser. The contract arranged for the foundry to produce military vehicles for

This photograph (taken around 1929) shows the marketplace and town gate of Günzberg, Germany, where the Mengele family owned a foundry. Even during the German depression, the Mengeles did well financially and employed many local workers. To this day, the town boasts a street with Karl Mengele's name.

the war effort. The Mengeles were able to indulge their nationalist feelings and make a handsome profit as well.

One of Josef's favorite things to do was to ride the horses that were used to deliver the military vehicles to the railway. The army wagons were destined for the war front. At an early age, Josef was well aware of his family's contribution to the war effort. At the end of the war in 1918, when many businesses went under, the Mengele foundry easily returned to the peacetime production of farm machinery.

Because of the demands of running a business, Josef's parents were often absent from his life. In his memoirs, Mengele wrote that his father was a cold man and that his mother was not very good at showing love. Josef learned that relationships within his family were not based on love but on respect. Josef grew to respect his mother's strong will and decisiveness. When his parents were around, the three brothers competed for their parents' attention. Josef developed a strong yearning for attention and fame because of the rivalry.

Many of Josef's early years were spent with his nanny, Monika. She was a devout Catholic who did not allow Josef—a curious youth—to question the Catholic faith. Josef was reminded that he was named after the father of Christ, like many of his relatives had been. Despite the strictness and lack

The Mengele foundry employed many workers in the town of Günzberg, and the family name was practically synonymous with farming equipment. Mengele's family maintained the foundry well after World War II, and it continues to operate today.

of love in Josef's life, he was known as a fun-loving child. In his memoirs, Mengele revealed that his sunny personality might have been a mask to cover deep inner suffering and unhappiness.

As a teenager, Josef was able to find some happiness by doing well in school. Although he wasn't at the top of his classes, Josef earned praise from his teachers for his self-discipline and self-control. He was a well-behaved student earning high marks for conduct and punctuality. His favorite subjects in school were biology, physics, and zoology. His favorite subject—one that became part of his life's work—was anthropology. Anthropology is the study of humans.

Josef developed into what many people thought was a striking, well-rounded teen. He was charming, confident, and comfortable with people. He had highly developed social skills for his age. He maintained a well-groomed appearance and wore tailored clothes from an early age. Josef also became a member of the Jugendbund—a patriotic German youth movement. Few could have predicted how dangerous the combination of young Josef's patriotism with his interest in anthropology would be.

CHAPTER TWO

RISE OF THE NAZI PARTY

I n the wake of the Great War, Josef's family found success with its foundry. The Mengele foundry had become one of the largest farming equipment manufacturers in Germany. The Mengele family dominated the town of Günzburg. The refined and intelligent Josef enjoyed his popularity, but also yearned to make a name for himself outside of his family's greatness. He not only wanted to succeed but also wanted fame.

Just before 1920, the swastika, a symbol soon to be used by the Nazis, made its appearance in Munich, a city in which Mengele would soon reside. The Thule Society, a conservative political organization, decided to use the symbol in an attempt to unite people behind the idea of German nationalism. Munich soon became the center for new political groups. Many new groups blamed Jews and foreigners for the German depression. Munich was also the place where the political strength of the future Nazi führer, or leader, Adolf Hitler, took root.

HITLER'S ENTRY INTO POLITICS

In 1919, a conservative political party was founded in Munich called the German Workers' Party (Deutsche Arbeiterpartei, or DAP). The goal of this party was the formation of a strong nationalist German state that would be influenced by middle-class interests. The hope was also that the German state would be entirely purged of Jews. Adolf Hitler attended a DAP meeting and decided to join. There were about fifty members at the time.

Hitler was a fiery speaker who set the DAP apart from other nationalist groups. Within a year, because of Hitler's ability to move his audiences, nearly 2,000 people were attending meetings. As early as 1920, Hitler was demanding that the citizenship of German Jews be taken away. He preached that Germany should be a vast Aryan empire void of non-Aryans and foreigners. He also called for the breaking of the Versailles Treaty. Hitler's words struck a chord in many Germans, and by 1921, over 6,000 people were attending the meetings. The DAP changed its name to the National-

sozialistische Deutsche Arbeiterpartei, or the
National Socialist German Workers' Party. Its
members soon became known as Nazis, which
is short for Nationalsozialistische.

At this 1925 party meeting in Munich, several notable Nazi leaders can be identified. Among them are Alfred Rosenberg (*left, with arms crossed*), Adolf Hitler (*standing, center*), and Heinrich Himmler (*far right*).

Hitler worked hard to develop his propaganda by studying racial and political theories. When Hitler developed his philosophy of national socialism, hatred of Jews was not new, but Hitler calling for the destruction of Jewish influence was new. Over the next few years, Hitler continued to campaign for the Nazi cause.

Hitler's group established many military-like divisions, including the Sturmabteilung, or Storm Troopers (SA), which Josef Mengele would join eleven years later. Members of the SA, also known as the Brown Shirts, were notorious for attacking Jews and anyone who spoke against Hitler or the Nazis.

In 1923, Hitler was injured and arrested during a Nazi attempt to overthrow the Bavarian government. He was put on trial, which brought national attention to him and the Nazi party. He accepted full responsibility for the failed overthrow and managed to use the attention from the trial to further Nazi propaganda.

Hitler was sentenced to five years in prison, of which he served only nine months. While he was in prison, he dictated his political manifesto, *Mein Kampf* (My Struggle). *Mein Kampf* became one of the twentieth century's most influential works, selling millions of copies in less than ten years. The work had a huge influence on many Germans and made desperately needed promises during a time of German economic and political weakness.

Mein Kampf emphasized Social Darwinism and racial theory. Hitler advanced the idea that some races create civilization while other races destroy it. He stated that the Jews were a destructive race that had to be removed from Germany. During the next six years, Hitler and the Nazi party spread their beliefs through rigorous campaigning and by attacking all political opposition.

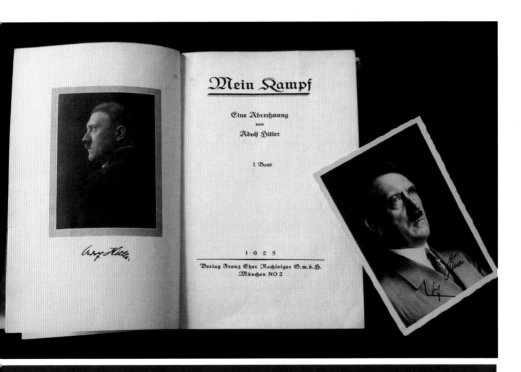

A signed first edition copy of Adolf Hitler's Nazi manifesto, Mein Kampf. The book, which promoted Social Darwinism and anti-Semitic racial theory, became highly influential as a propaganda tool against Jews in Germany.

MENGELE'S UNIVERSITY STUDIES

Mengele passed his school exams in 1930. Being the eldest son, he was first in line to work at the family business. But Mengele was driven by his desire to make a name for himself, so he looked into other careers. At one point, he considered becoming a dentist, since his town lacked one. He reasoned that he would be highly valued and respected.

Ultimately, Mengele decided on medicine. He had been influenced by Germany's interest in eugenics and racial theory, and decided to focus his studies on anthropology and human genetics. He told a friend that by focusing on these fields, he could study the entire range of medicine. A wave of interest in genetics was sweeping through the intellectual world, and Mengele hoped to make his mark. He also hoped that by becoming the first scientist in his family, he would earn the respect of his parents.

Mengele left his family and moved to Munich in October 1930 in order to attend Munich University. Munich was brimming with Nazi activity at the time. The movement had spread throughout the rest of Germany as well. The Nazis had become the second-largest political party in the German parliament. Mengele was fully exposed to the Nazi movement. He took a keen interest in the philosophies of Alfred Rosenberg, a philosopher of the Nazi

Alfred Rosenberg's philosophy on race and German nationalism was central to the Nazi party's anti-Semitic racial policies. Rosenberg became a prominent party member and had a strong influence on Josef Mengele's ideas on anthropology and genetics.

movement. In 1930, Rosenberg published his book *The Myth of the Twentieth Century*, which sold millions of copies. His book promoted the racist idea that Germans must keep German blood pure from racial contamination. Sixteen years later, Rosenberg would be hanged for crimes against humanity.

At university, Mengele showed more of an interest in learning about evolution and cultural origins than in treating the ill. In addition to his studies, Josef was attracted to political issues. In 1931, he joined the youth wing of the Stahlhelm, or Steel Helmets, at the age of twenty. The Steel Helmets was a nationalistic, anti-Semitic group founded in 1918 by World War I veterans. Mengele liked the group's military style and strong sense of nationalism. On October 11, 1931, an alliance was formed between the Nazis, the Steel Helmets, and other nationalist groups, with the goal of making Germany a dominant empire, free of what they considered racial burdens.

During the same year that Josef Mengele joined the Steel Helmets, his father, Karl, decided to join the Nazi party. The senior Mengele saw a bright future for the Nazi movement. One of his companions was the chief of the local Nazi party, which had driven out the roughly three hundred Jews who lived in Günzburg. Karl Mengele's involvement in the Nazi party brought Hitler to Günzburg a year later for a speech at the Mengele factory. In the years to follow, Karl Mengele was made a town council member and his business boomed, employing more than three hundred fifty people, all thanks to his Nazi connections.

HITLER'S RISE TO POWER

By 1933, Adolf Hitler was named chancellor of Germany. The German parliament hoped that by giving him this position, Hitler could be controlled and a Nazi overthrow of the parliament could be avoided. In this position, however, Hitler was able to change the system from within. By the end of 1933, many laws were passed that would help the Nazis to establish the Third Reich.

The Third Reich, which means the third kingdom, was the name for Germany under Nazi control. The Nazis viewed the Holy Roman Empire (which existed from the early Middle Ages until 1806) as the First Reich and the German Empire (1871–1918) as the Second Reich. Hitler wanted the Third Reich to dominate Europe. He envisioned that the so-called lesser races would be used as slave laborers for the master Aryan race.

Many scientists and academics helped Hitler develop his national socialist philosophies into laws. One of these scientists, Dr. Ernst Rudin, was a strong influence on Josef Mengele. Mengele regularly attended Dr. Rudin's lectures while at school. Rudin helped draw up the sterilization laws that Hitler enacted in July 1933.

Rudin held the radical belief that doctors should destroy any life that had no value. Rudin believed that people had no value if they suffered from alcoholism, blindness, deafness, epilepsy, mental disorders, physical malformations,

Shown here at a Nazi political rally in 1933, Hitler was an incredibly charismatic and lively speaker—an attribute that helped him influence and indoctrinate German masses with official Nazi party ideology. Hitler relied heavily on doctors such as Josef Mengele and Alfred Rosenberg to craft his party's policies on race.

mental slowness, or disease. He hoped that by killing people with these characteristics, the quality of the German race would improve. This was also known as "racial hygiene." Mengele was exposed to many respected professionals whose beliefs on race reflected Dr. Rudin's views.

THE FIRST CONCENTRATION CAMP

Hitler established the first concentration camp, Dachau, within the first few months of 1933. The purpose of the concentration camp was to imprison anyone who opposed the Third Reich. It was also a place where Hitler could send the undesirables or "asocials" of German society. Asocials were those people who were deemed to be a burden or harmful to German society.

The first inmates of the camp were Communists, Democrats, and Jews with powerful

A chart explains the identification badges used for the various types of prisoners sent to concentration camps. Different colored badges identified political prisoners, Jehovah's Witnesses, homosexuals, and other "asocials." A Star of David identified Jewish inmates.

jobs such as officials, journalists, and lawyers. The so-called asocials who were sent there included criminals, homosexuals, alcoholics, Jehovah's Witnesses, beggars, vagrants, and mentally and physically challenged people. The concentration camp was meant to ensure that the Nazis would not be opposed in their drive to control all of Germany.

Hitler also quickly established harsh racial policies. The Nazis developed a nationwide system of defining Jewish ancestry on the basis of a German's bloodline. People with both German and Jewish ancestors were called *Mischlinge*, or half-breeds. There were immediate boycotts on all Jewish and *Mischling* shops and businesses. Jews were forced to quit all civil service jobs and important positions. Jews were turned away from school and denied basic liberties. Hitler started Aryanization, which was the taking over of Jewish businesses and jobs by non-Jewish Germans.

As Mengele was studying medicine, German Nazi leaders were looking to those with medical expertise to make the new Germany a reality. By 1934, Hitler established the racial hygiene policy throughout Germany. A sterilization law was created, called the Law for the Prevention of Genetically Diseased Offspring, which made all doctors responsible for reporting and sterilizing all Germans with genetic defects.

The German president died in 1934, allowing Hitler to assume total power over Germany. Soon it

MISCHLING TEST

In 1935, Hitler designed two new race-based measures to deny Jews living in Germany of basic rights. These laws, commonly called the Nuremberg Laws, stripped Jews of German citizenship and outlawed marriage or sexual relations between Jews and non-Jewish Germans.

However, shortly after the laws passed, it became problematic that there was no clear definition provided in the law of who was a "Jew" and who was a "German." The Nazi party quickly delineated two categories of Jews: *Jude* and *Mischling*.

A *Jude*, or full-blood Jew, was any individual with at least three Jewish grandparents. A *Mischling*, or "cross-breed," fell into one of two categories. First-degree *Mischlinge* had two Jewish grandparents, but did not practice Judaism. Second-degree *Mischlinge* had only one Jewish grandparent.

The racist policies encouraged Germans to hire genealogists and prove the so-called purity of their non-Jewish ancestry. The Health Ministry kept close track of records and enforced the Nuremberg Laws accordingly.

After passing the Nuremberg Laws of 1935, the Nazi party quickly had to clarify who was and who was not a Jew. The above chart became a popular aid in determining the "purity" of one's German ancestry.

was accepted that some lives were not worth living, or that some people were unworthy of life. Along with the sterilization law, a euthanasia program was developed in order to free Germany from taking care of the unworthy. People deemed worthless were killed in the euthanasia program. This was cruelly believed to relieve these people of their suffering. Hitler's emphasis on a medical solution to Germany's problems brought those in the medical profession to the forefront. Many of Josef Mengele's teachers were swept up in the powerful force of the Nazi movement; soon Mengele would be as well.

MENGELE JOINS THE NAZI PARTY

Mengele worked ambitiously for a doctorate in anthropology while also pursuing a degree in medicine. Between 1934 and 1938, Mengele wrote papers on heredity and genetics in relation to racial groups. Although his thinking was right in line with Nazi ideas on race and genetics, his works were surprisingly void of anti-Semitic themes. The papers were more scientific than racist.

In 1936, Mengele passed his final examinations in Munich. He landed his first paid job in the university medical clinic at Leipzig. Mengele worked long hours as a beginning doctor but still found the time to fall in love. He met a professor's daughter named Irene Schönbein, his future first wife and mother of his son, Rolf. Life as a doctor did not please Mengele. He yearned to return to his research studies in genetics. On the recommendation of a Leipzig professor, Mengele was transferred to the Third Reich's Institute of Hereditary Biology and Race Research.

At the institute, he was given a research assistant position under one of Europe's most important genetic scientists, Otmar Freiherr von Verschuer. Dr. von Verschuer founded the institute in 1934. Dr. von Verschuer was an admirer of Hitler and the role of medicine in the Third Reich. Von Verschuer believed that the science of eugenics would come to full bloom under Nazi leadership. The young,

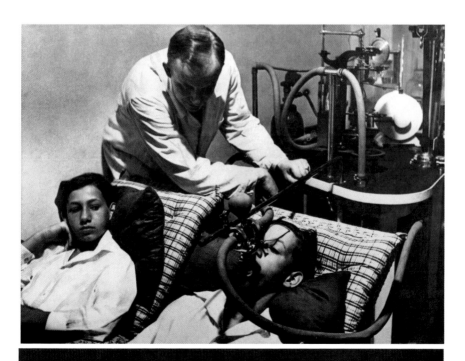

At the Institute of Hereditary Biology and Race Research, Dr. Otmar Freiherr von Verschuer carried out a number of experiments on genetics. His particular interest in twins would be passed on to his most infamous disciple, Josef Mengele.

twenty-six-year-old Mengele developed a strong respect for Dr. von Verschuer's beliefs, which undoubtedly influenced Mengele to follow his urge to join the Nazi party.

After a four-year ban on joining the Nazi Party, Mengele was allowed to apply in 1937. Hitler had restricted membership in the party in 1933 because he feared that too many liberals would want to join. He believed that these people would weaken the party's strength. After being accepted by the Nazi Party, Mengele applied for membership in the most elite group of the party, the SS, or Schutzstaffel, which means protection squad. The SS controlled all German police agencies and was responsible for guarding Germany's racial purity. Mengele's family history was inspected, and after it became clear to the Nazis that he was a "pure" German, he was allowed to join.

Although all SS members were ordered to get a tattoo signifying their membership and blood type, Josef managed to avoid the tattoo. He did not want his perfect skin to be marred. He also joined the National Socialist German Doctors' League (Nationalsozialistischer Deutscher Ärztebund, or NSDÄB), which was the Nazi physicians' association. Membership in the Nazi Party complemented his research work at the institute, which was to study the importance of heredity in relation to the Nazi goal of racial hygiene.

CHAPTER THREE

BECOMING THE NAZI DOCTOR

By the end of 1938, Mengele had joined the ranks of the Nazi Party and become a licensed doctor of medicine. His prior work at the Institute of Hereditary Biology and Race Research had remained in line with Nazi ideology on race and genetics, but in order to assure his success as a member of the SS, Mengele left his post at the institute and attended three months of training with the German army. When training ended, he was sent to his first posting in the Snalfedon-Tirol mountain region, where he served until the end of his posting. He then returned to his research work.

In 1939, Mengele married Irene after a Nazi search into her ancestral background had been conducted. The race of her grandfather was not known, and it was proposed that he might be Jewish. Irene's Aryan appearance, with blond hair and Nordic features, finally swayed officials to allow the marriage. Mengele was disappointed that he could not prove Irene's Aryan ancestry. This meant that their names wouldn't be added to a Nazi book called *Sippenbuch*, or kinship book. Inclusion in the book indicated that an SS member's family was racially pure and Aryan.

While finishing his studies in Frankfurt, Mengele also wrote reviews of academic books about heredity. He asserted that many of the books did not place enough emphasis on the superiority of the German race. Mengele was now completely under the power of the Nazi movement. He believed that Hitler was the one man who could save the human race from self-destruction. A few weeks after Mengele's wedding in 1939, Hitler started a war in the belief that he could do just that.

KRISTALLNACHT AND JEWISH GHETTOS

During the years that Mengele spent at the institute, Hitler was able to bring all aspects of German life under Nazi domination. The German police and all government offices were under Nazi control. He established Nazi schools for the German youth, so Nazi education could start early. Hitler also worked to dehumanize Jews and asocials; if his followers saw Jews and "asocials" as less than human, it would be easier to get rid of them. The sterilization and euthanasia programs were expanded so that tens of thousands of patients could be treated for racial hygiene.

On November 9, 1938, an attack on the remaining Jewish populations in Germany, Austria, and parts of Czechoslovakia occurred. Jewish people were assaulted and murdered, and Jewish businesses and synagogues were burned. This attack is called Kristallnacht, or the "Night of Broken Glass." It marked the murderous beginning of Hitler's solution to Germany's problems. Over thirty thousand Jewish men were sent to concentration camps during Kristallnacht.

Kristallnacht, or the "Night of Broken Glass," marked an escalation in anti-Semitic violence in Nazi Germany. Shown here are the ruins of the Tielshafer Synagogue in Berlin, which was burned by Nazis on Kristallnacht.

Aside from ridding the German Empire of Jews and the so-called asocials, another of Hitler's goals was that Germany would acquire land from neighboring territories. He felt that the German people needed and deserved more *Lebensraum*, or living space. Conquered territories would provide extra space for living and farming. Having more territory would also help the Third Reich assure its dominance over Europe. Of course, this land wouldn't be handed over freely; it would have to be taken by force.

Germany had already annexed Austria and Czechoslovakia, and on September 1, 1939, Hitler and the German army invaded Poland. This was the start of World War II. Two days later, Great Britain and France declared war on Germany because of its move against Poland. When Germany took over Poland, it also inherited the two million Jews who lived there. As more territories were conquered, more Jews and "asocials" would have to be dealt with. Within a month of the invasion, plans to establish ghettos throughout Poland were underway.

Ghettos were heavily guarded, enclosed sub-cities that were designed to hold people that Hitler wanted removed from the German Empire. All Jews of conquered territories would be sent to the ghettos and then on to concentration camps. Ghettos were overcrowded and unsanitary. Jews in the ghettos were forced to wear armbands that marked their Jewish identity. Anyone caught without an armband was executed immediately.

In October 1939, Hitler established an area in Poland to serve as an administrative center of government for the conquered territory. In the not-too-distant future, the Nazis would build many of their death camps in this area. Death

A 1944 map published by underground resistance forces in Poland marks the locations of many of the Nazi concentration camps that were established during the German occupation. Nazis used these camps to solve overcrowding issues in Jewish ghettos.

camps were a key part of the Nazi plan to destroy Jews and "asocials." These camps were used for large-scale murder.

Josef Mengele stands at a train window in his Schutzstaffel (SS) uniform. Taken about 1945, this photograph is one of very few that survive of Mengele during his

MENGELE BECOMES A SOLDIER

At the outbreak of the war, Mengele was suffering from a kidney ailment. His health condition forced him to wait until July 1940 before joining the war service. He saw the war as Germany's chance to create a dominant Aryan empire. His first post was as a medical officer in an army unit. A month later, Mengele transferred to a special wing of the SS called the Waffen SS, which was the largest branch of the SS. Waffen SS members were soldiers who fought at the war front, seeing much bloodshed.

During the first few months of 1941, Mengele was stationed in occupied Poland, where he worked at the Race and Resettlement Office. He worked under the direct orders of Heinrich Himmler. Himmler was the leader of the entire SS. He was a very powerful man in the Nazi movement who also oversaw the camps. Himmler believed that Germany would be rid of the Jewish problem once Germany exterminated all Jews. He felt that killing Jews was a German right.

Prior to the German occupation of Poland, the Nazis had established a division of the SS called the SS Einsatzgruppen, or action squads. The Einsatzgruppen were well-armed, mobile murdering squads. During the invasion of Poland,

GENERALPLAN OST (GPO)

As Nazi Germany occupied territories east of its established border, it faced the issue of how to deal with Jews and other non-Germans that were gradually annexed into its boundaries. Nazi leaders created a plan for how to ethnically cleanse the Eastern European territories Germany occupied during World War II. This plan was the Generalplan Ost ("Master Plan East," or GPO). Heinrich Himmler instructed Mengele and other SS doctors to determine the racial strength of the Polish people in the newly conquered territories. The Nazis would allow only pro-Nazi, non-Jewish Polish people of German descent to live in these territories. Poles believed to be the descendants of German colonists or settlers were to be Germanized and integrated into the German population. About 1.7 million Polish peoples were determined to be Germanizable.

First Poles and, later, Slavs living in German-conquered territories who were not determined to be Germanizable were to be enslaved, expelled, or exterminated in accordance with the Generalplan Ost. In the period following a presumed victory in World War II, Himmler and the Nazis planned on removing approximately 45 million non-Germanizable people from Central and Eastern Europe. Doctors with an understanding of race and genetics and unwavering support for Nazi beliefs (such as Josef Mengele) would be an essential part of this plan. Their expertise was needed to examine and determine the so-called racial purity of conquered peoples.

they were used to kill hundreds of Polish Jews and Catholic intellectuals. The units were assigned to kill anyone who was not racially "pure" or who posed a threat to the Nazi Empire.

In June 1941, Germany invaded the Soviet Union. Three thousand Einsatzgruppen soldiers entered the Soviet Union to kill Jews and Russian officials rather than transport them to ghettos or camps. The Einsatzgruppen soldiers were known for their ruthless massacres, witnessed by many with horror. Many of these killings were brutal and sadistic, such as smashing children's skulls against walls while swinging them by their ankles. The Einsatzgruppen were responsible for more than one million Jewish deaths during the Holocaust. Many members of other German troop divisions, including the Waffen SS, were invited and encouraged to witness the brutal killings carried out by the Einsatzgruppen.

At the time of the invasion of the Soviet Union, Mengele was posted to service in Ukraine,

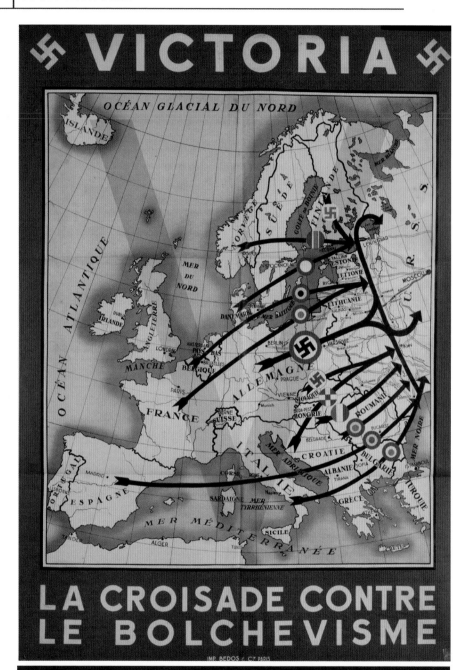

After the invasion of the Soviet Union in June 1941, Nazi propaganda was distributed throughout Germany and German-occupied territory to rally support for the war efforts. This poster from Nazi-occupied France promotes "the crusade against Bolshevism," or communism.

which was part of the Soviet Union. Within just a few days of his posting there, Mengele was awarded a medal called the Iron Cross for his actions during dangerous battlefield conditions. Mengele was transferred to the medical corps of the Waffen SS Viking division in January 1942. This division went further into Russian territory than any other German army unit.

By July, Mengele's division had moved up to the front line for a bloody battle against the Russian army that lasted five days. Mengele was awarded another medal for his soldiering during this battle. He was awarded a first class Iron Cross for rescuing two German soldiers from a burning tank. While fighting on the Russian front, Mengele was injured. Due to his injury, Mengele was declared unfit for further action.

In late 1942, Mengele was transferred to Berlin to work at the Race and Resettlement Office. By this time, he had been decorated with four war medals— two Iron Crosses, the Black Badge for the Wounded, and the Medal for the Care of the German People. He was the only Nazi doctor to have earned such a collection of medals and was promoted to the rank of *Hauptsturmführer*, or captain.

THE FINAL SOLUTION

While Mengele was serving in the Waffen SS, plans for the Final Solution were being developed in the German Third Reich. The Final Solution was a

Heinrich Himmler was a high-ranking member of the Nazi party as well as the individual believed to be most responsible for the development of the Final Solution. Himmler was also the SS chief under whom Josef Mengele served in Poland.

horrific plan that the Nazis believed would rid Germany of Jews forever. The plan outlined the systematic murder of every single European Jew. It was often referred to as "the Final Solution to the Jewish question."

Although historians aren't sure of the exact date on which the Final Solution started, documents recovered long after World War II offer proof that it began in June 1941. The first public mention of the Final Solution occurred ten years earlier in a newspaper article in the *Munich Post*, but it suggested a different means to that end. The Final Solution of 1931 was a plan to remove Jews from German society through slave labor.

Heinrich Himmler—under whom Mengele served in Poland—played a key role in the creation of the Final Solution plan of 1941. A year earlier, in May 1940, he drew up a memorandum that called for the removal of Jews by any means necessary. It stated that extermination of Jews was not impossible. By using the term "extermination" rather than the word "murder," Himmler furthered the idea that Jews were subhuman and that it was acceptable to kill them. The memorandum was given to Hitler, who read the paper and authorized it to become a directive. Hitler asked Himmler to notify key Nazi leaders of the new directive.

The idea of the Final Solution was passed to Hermann Göring, a leading member of the Nazi Party. Göring then authorized Reinhard Heydrich, another Nazi leader, to carry out the Final Solution to the Jewish question. The Final Solution was to be used in all parts of German-dominated Europe.

No written details were ever found that stated how Hitler wished the Final Solution to be carried out. Historians assume that Hitler's right-hand men did their best to interpret how he wanted it done. This included the increased action of the killing squads, more efforts to establish death camps, and the deportation of Jews to death camps for immediate extermination. By the end of the year, several death camps were in full operation and had already carried out the murder of several thousand Jews, Roma, prisoners of war, and other "asocials."

CHAPTER FOUR

AUSCHWITZ'S ANGEL OF DEATH

As they advanced across Europe, the Nazi troops—and in particular, the SS and the Einsatzgruppen—carried out gruesome attacks. Children and other innocent civilians were not killed instantly; they were often shot and left in pain, or brutally assaulted. Many German soldiers had difficulty coping with their task. Several members committed suicide rather than live with the knowledge of what they had done. It soon became obvious to Nazi leaders that the responsibility for carrying out the Final Solution was too much for young soldiers to bear as they swept across Eastern Europe. Nazi leaders sought out less gruesome ways to murder the Nazi enemies. They turned their efforts toward the death camps and looked for more methodical ways to kill.

MENGELE HEADS TO AUSCHWITZ

In the summer of 1942, Mengele's old friend and mentor Dr. von Verschuer was named director of the Kaiser Wilhelm Institute for Anthropology, Human Genetics, and Eugenics in Berlin. This was a few months before Mengele's transfer to Berlin. As director of the institute, von Verschuer oversaw research programs for German racial purity. Many of the research projects involved the use of twins in order to have a way of comparing test results. Mengele soon contacted von Verschuer and said that he would work at the institute during his free time while posted in Berlin.

The Final Solution was well underway by the time Mengele reached Berlin. The Nazis did not publicize their plans for the Final Solution. The purpose of the secrecy was to get full cooperation from everyone, especially the victims. The Nazi doctors, however, did know of the concentration and death camps, and several Nazi doctors were already experimenting on camp prisoners. Soon the Nazi doctors would become a crucial part of the Final Solution.

It's likely that von Verschuer encouraged the thirty-two-year-old Mengele to apply for a post at Auschwitz, the largest concentration death camp. Mengele would have an unlimited supply of test subjects there and the freedom to carry out any kind of research project. Furthermore, Mengele would have access to a group of people that was very important to his and von Verschuer's research—twins.

Mengele arrived at Auschwitz on May 30, 1943. Soon after Mengele's arrival, von Verschuer

Otmar Freiherr von Verschuer is shown sorting through files at the Kaiser Wilhelm Institute for Anthropology, Human Genetics, and Eugenics in Berlin. Von Verschuer's encouragement led Mengele to apply for his post at Auschwitz in 1943.

applied for and received grants for the studies that he and Mengele would continue carrying out. Mengele would send specimens from Auschwitz to von Verschuer in Berlin, and their research work would continue.

The Auschwitz camp was a nightmarish world unto itself. The construction of the Auschwitz concentration camp began in 1940. Over the next five years, a forced labor camp and a death camp were built. The camp was located in the town where the former Polish military had trained, so it was already well suited to house many people. The camp was also located near the major railroad lines of Poland, so trains loaded with prisoners would have easy access.

From 1940 until 1945, the Auschwitz concentration camp operated as one of Nazi Germany's deadliest forced labor camps. Its entry gate opened under a sign that read *"Arbeit macht frei,"* German for "Work makes you free."

The camp spread out over a few miles and had three main sections. Auschwitz I was the concentration and main camp. Auschwitz II, also called Auschwitz-Birkenau, was the death camp. Auschwitz III, also called Monowitz-Buna, was a forced-labor camp. There were also several sub-camps located within a few miles of the enormous Auschwitz camp.

WORKING IN THE DEATH CAMPS

Nazi leaders decided that death by gassing was the least gruesome and most efficient way to extermi-nate large groups of prisoners at once. Death camps were established to carry out the gassings with efficiency. From the *Selektionen* (German for "Selections"—the process by which new inmates were chosen for work labor, medical experimenta-tion, or death) to the disposal of corpses, the Nazi doctors were involved at every stage of the gassings.

Most Nazi doctors at Auschwitz, except for doctors who had specific duties such as taking care of SS members, were required to take part in the gassings. Nazi leaders and doctors designed the stages of the gassings to be misleading to the prisoners. Every action that the Nazi soldiers and doctors performed was part of a cruel hoax that lead the prisoners quickly and quietly to their death.

Upon exiting the train at Auschwitz, the prisoners formed a line for the *Selektionen*. When a prisoner was chosen by a Nazi doctor to go to the left, the prisoner was told that he or she would be taking a shower in the bathhouse. Many of the doctors on duty at the *Selektionen* made a show of acting polite and pretended to be concerned for the well-being of the prisoners.

Prisoners were instructed to follow the line to the bathhouse. Those too weak to walk were put into vehicles. After the *Selektionen* was finished, the *Selektionen* doctor was driven to the building where the gassings took place. The doctor was driven in a vehicle painted with a red cross to make it appear as though medical professionals were carrying out a humane procedure. Another part of the hoax was that other prisoners from the labor camp were selected to help in the process. It seemed impossible that prisoners would lead other prisoners to their deaths, but in order to avoid their own death, they did so by the thousands.

Once the prisoners were lured into the building marked "bathhouse," the building was locked from the outside. The doctor determined how many pellets of gas would be needed to kill the prisoners. The doctor also selected one officer out of a special group called disinfectors. A disinfector was a medical technician whose duty was to drop the poisonous pellets inside the locked chamber. The doctor would sometimes observe how the prisoners were dying.

A memorial stands inside the main gas chamber at the former site of the Auschwitz concentration camp. Countless prisoners were brought into this chamber to be mercilessly killed. The corpses were then cremated to hide evidence of the atrocities.

After the prisoners were dead, the doctor gave the order to open and air out the chamber. He then noted the amount of time that it had taken for the prisoners to die and signed a form verifying their deaths. Lastly, the doctor made sure that the bodies were burned in the crematorium. The crematorium was connected to the gas chamber. Burning the bodies was done in part to erase the evidence that millions of murders were taking place.

On a clear day, the billowing smoke of burning bodies from the crematoriums could be seen thirty miles from Auschwitz. The burning flesh produced a constant stench, which Mengele's wife asked about when she visited the camp. Mengele told Irene not to ask about such matters, which abruptly ended discussion of the sickening smell of Auschwitz.

The gassings occurred several times a day during the twenty months that Mengele served at Auschwitz. During this time, Mengele not only presided over his own *Selektionen*, but he would often show up even when he wasn't scheduled for selections. Survivors of Auschwitz remember that Mengele was one of the few doctors who didn't need liquor or drugs to help him get through the selection process. Many doctors reported to duty drunk or high in an attempt to cope with the *Selektionen* tasks. Mengele showed up for *Selektionen* duty with enthusiasm, even though the process sent hundreds of thousands of people to their deaths.

MENGELE EXCELS AT AUSCHWITZ

In a place where the doctors were expected to cause death, there was little that Mengele could do to fail. In fact, Mengele excelled in the environment of Auschwitz. He took on any extra challenges that he could. He proved that he fully agreed with the Nazi movement and its Final Solution. He also proved that he had no problems using the gas chambers to solve any situations that came up.

Within a month of Mengele's arrival, the Roma prisoner camp had an outbreak of typhus, which is a disease that spreads quickly. (The Roma, or Romani, people are a nomadic ethnic group that has lived in Europe and the Americas for centuries. They are often called "Gypsies," although that name is considered offensive.) Mengele's solution was to send more than one thousand Roma to the gas chambers. He spared only Roma of German ancestry. Nazis didn't hate the Roma as much as Jews but still saw them as a threat to an ordered way of life. There are conflicting reports about how Mengele felt about Roma people. Some people believe that he was kind to

Because of poor nutrition and substandard living condiitons, prisoners at Nazi concentration camps, such as these Roma women, were prone to outbreaks of disease such as typhus. Mengele swiftly dealt with such outbreaks by killing all infected prisoners.

them, while others—who cite this mass killing as an example—say that Mengele hated the Roma as much as he hated the Jews.

A few months later, the women's camp also had an outbreak of typhus. Mengele sent all the Jewish inhabitants of one barrack—more than six hundred women—to the gas chamber. He did this to cleanse the barracks of typhus. He then moved other infected women in to treat them in the clean barracks. He had each emptied barrack completely "cleansed" in order to rid the camp of typhus. During this time, he became infected with typhus himself, but soon recovered. Chief SS doctor Eduard Wirths felt that Mengele deserved the War Service Medal for finding a solution to the typhus epidemic.

ANGEL OF DEATH: A SYMBOL OF AUSCHWITZ

Many survivors remember Mengele as a horrible figure who came to symbolize Auschwitz. Others remember that in contrast to the weak, dirty prisoners, Mengele, with his immaculate, pristine composure, stood out like a movie star. In survivors' and colleagues' memories, Mengele ranges from being a murderous madman to a gentleman. Many people believe that Mengele was both. His upbringing had given him what appeared to be a refined nature, while his reverence for the Nazis allowed him to heartlessly follow grisly orders.

THE INNOCENT DOCTOR OF AUSCHWITZ

Dr. Miklós Nyiszli was a Hungarian-Jewish prisoner of Auschwitz who had the misfortune of knowing and working with Josef Mengele. Upon arrival at the concentration camp, Nyiszli volunteered his services as a doctor, and doctors were needed to help with the Nazis' medical experiments. Thus, Nyiszli was spared death and assigned to assist in human experimentation.

When Mengele first arrived at Auschwitz, he asked Nyiszli to accompany him on a tour through the camp. Up until that point, Nyiszli had only seen the small section of the camp in which he was forced to live. When Mengele showed him the rest of the camp, Nyiszli was both amazed and terrified by the size of Auschwitz. At the time of Mengele's arrival, Auschwitz held more than 130,000 prisoners, and exterminated over 5,000 people a day.

During Nyiszli's eight-month stay at Auschwitz, he witnessed countless deaths and was forced to perform inhumane procedures and autopsies against his will. After two transfers to other concentration camps as Allied Forces closed in on German-occupied territory, Dr. Nyiszli was freed by U.S. soldiers on May 5, 1945. He died on the same date, twelve years later. In 1960, his writings on his time in Auschwitz were published as *Auschwitz: A Doctor's Eyewitness Account*. In 2001, the book was adapted into the film *The Grey Zone*.

Sixteen months into his posting at Auschwitz, the chief physician evaluated Mengele's work. Mengele was commended for his outstanding service. The evaluation went on to say that even though Mengele was a strict soldier, he was also popular and respected by his SS peers. There is little doubt that Mengele enjoyed his duties. He conducted the *Selektionen* with precision and speed. He uttered "right" or "left" within a few seconds of seeing each prisoner. One prisoner called him "the Lord of life or death." Soon, he was commonly known as the Angel of Death. His military record separated him from other Nazi doctors who had no war experience. He wore his war medals proudly and kept military bearing and behavior.

Auschwitz leaders made life in the camps as comfortable as possible for Nazi officers such as Mengele. There were orchestras made up of prisoner musicians that played during the *Selektionen*

In 2007, the United States Holocaust Memorial Museum obtained the Höcker Album, a rare collection of photographs that documented the lives of Nazi officers at Auschwitz. Eight photographs in the collection featured Mengele (shown here, far left).

and throughout the camp. The orchestras were used both to make the prisoners believe that it was a peaceful camp and to entertain the Nazi officers. The camp also had a swimming pool, theater, library, soccer stadium, and bar—all for SS soldiers only. A few Nazi leaders had their families living within the camp in nice homes. Some Nazi families even tended gardens and kept pets.

Although some survivors remember Mengele as being almost everywhere at once, Mengele had his own laboratory block and his own medical staff. The staff was mostly made up of prisoners who had medical expertise, such as technicians, nurses, and doctors. He was not overly kind to his staff—many of them were Jews. Occasionally, however, he lost sight of that fact and treated some of them as colleagues. They had lively discussions about the nature of the research and the findings from the studies. But one wrong word in the conversation and Mengele would return to treating staff members like subhumans.

Even with his duties of *Selektionen* and his own research, Mengele found time to take part in the labor camp activities. After selections, about two out of every fifteen people were sent to the labor camp. The rest (thirteen out of every fifteen) were sent to the gas chambers. Those who made it to the labor camp were literally worked to death. Many strong-spirited prisoners worked well past exhaustion. Labor camp selections were established in order to weed out exhausted workers as their energy drained away.

During labor camp selections, prisoners were forced to stand in organized lines for hours, sometimes in the freezing cold. At some selections, the prisoners were asked to undress completely so that the doctors could easily examine the prisoner's physical condition. Within a few seconds, the doctors decided which prisoners were to be sent to the gas chambers or to return to work. It was a morbid replaying of the moment when the prisoners had first arrived at Auschwitz. Just as he took particular joy in the initial *Selektionen*, Mengele participated frequently in the labor camp selections.

GETTING AWAY WITH MURDER

Even to do this day, few can imagine the extent of the atrocities that took place in the Nazi concentration camps. The mass killings, forced labor, and medical experimentation are simply beyond the scope of what most could ever believe. There were over seventy different medical research experiments done in the camps. More than two hundred Nazi doctors conducted experiments—some for military purposes and others for the purposes of racial hygiene. Military experiments were done to aid the German war effort. Racial experiments were done to try and scientifically prove that other races were inferior, to keep other races from breeding, and to advance the Aryan race.

In both types of experiments, prisoners became subjects against their will. Most of the experiments were brutal and done without painkillers. Some experiments were done merely to satisfy morbid medical curiosity, such as answering the question, "What if a human being were starved to death? How long might he or she remain alive?" Autopsies—examinations of deceased prisoners—were also a part of the experiments. This meant that the death of the patient was an expected stage of the experiment.

MILITARY EXPERIMENTS AT AUSCHWITZ

The Nazis made a great deal of effort to gain any advantage on the battlefield they could. The medical experiments on prisoners were done in the hopes of helping German soldiers survive on the front lines. The experiments did not always use modern medical techniques, often were brutal, and usually led to the deaths of the prisoners.

- **Amputations** Limbs of prisoners were cut off to see how fast blood flowed from live, alert humans. This was done in hopes of finding ways of slowing blood flow from wounds.
- **Freezing experiments** Prisoners were immersed in freezing water to see how long they could survive before dying.
- **Transplants** The limbs were cut off of two prisoners and switched to see if transplants could work.
- **Wound experiments** Prisoners were given wounds as well as bacterial infections to simulate wounds received at the battlefront. Patients were then treated with experimental medications in attempts to cure the infections.

UNETHICAL EXPERIMENTS

Mengele's experiments were conducted for purposes of racial hygiene and were as gruesome as the military experiments. Most of the survivors from Mengele's experiments are twins. He conducted research on twins of all ages because he hoped to unlock the secrets of multiple births. With this knowledge, it was hoped that Aryans could be born in multiple numbers, and the population could quickly increase as a result. Other experiments were carried out to understand genetics. More than forty sets of prisoner twins survived Mengele's experiments and the Holocaust.

Mengele went as far as to attend other doctors' *Selektionen* to make sure that twins were being spared from the gassings. Prisoners remember Mengele and other SS soldiers directing twins to step out of the *Selektionen*, shouting, "Twins, twins, out!" Twins were separated from the prisoners and placed in special barracks. Because they were part of the Nazi race studies, twins lived in better conditions than the labor camp prisoners. Mengele made sure that the twins he was studying were well fed and taken care of.

Eva Mozes Kor and her twin sister, Miriam, were two of Mengele's subjects at Auschwitz. In 1985, Eva spoke at a U.S. Senate subcommittee hearing to determine Mengele's whereabouts. After the Holocaust, Kor became an important advocate for other Holocaust survivors.

The twins were carefully measured, X-rayed, and examined. The measurements of one twin were compared to the measurements of the other. Each twin had a file filled with research data. Because Mengele's files were never found, it is not certain what the precise goals of each of his experiments were.

The last stage of the experiment was usually an autopsy. The twins were either gassed or injected with a poison called phenol. Mengele and his assistants administered the deadly shots. Phenol injections had been used earlier in the war to kill prisoners. After months of experimentation with the injections, the Nazis discovered that the quickest and easiest way of administering the shot was by stabbing a syringe directly into the heart. This method produced death within fifteen seconds.

Another of Mengele's bizarre experiments was focused on eye color. The ultimate Aryan was believed to have blond hair and blue eyes. Mengele started working on seven-year-old prisoners who had blond hair and brown eyes. He injected the prisoners' eyes with chemicals and dyes such as methylene blue to see if he could change the natural coloring of the eye's iris. Mengele also did the same experiment on twins and other prisoners. Some patients recovered from the injections, but others suffered infections, blindness, and, in one known case, death.

MENGELE'S EXPERIMENTS ON TWINS

Medical experiments on twins included but were not limited to the following:

- **Sampling** Great amounts of blood or tissue were taken from some sets of twins, which caused their deaths.
- **Blood transfusions** The blood of one set of twins was switched with the blood of another set of twins.
- **Organ switching** The organs of one twin were switched with those of the other twin, or one set's organs were switched with the organs of another set of twins.
- **Deliberate infection and poisoning** Twins were injected with diseases or poisons and their reactions were compared.

Mengele also experimented on prisoners who had physical abnormalities or were abnormally short. Mengele ordered soldiers to shoot the prisoners with physical abnormalities, and their bodies were examined. At one point, Mengele found an entire family of short people at the *Selektionen*. He was very kind to them during the experiments, but when the experiments came to an end, they were gassed. Mengele's research findings, along with the bones of the dead, were sent to von Verschuer for continued study.

Mengele also sent sets of eyes to von Verschuer that were taken from the bodies of the twins, Roma, and other "patients." Some prisoners were deliberately killed just to harvest the eye samples, especially any Roma prisoners with two different colored eyes. The samples of experiments and research material were always carefully packed and shipped off by Mengele's assistants. Survivors remember menacing collections of human eyes on tables and tacked to the walls of Mengele's laboratories.

Dr. Mengele also studied a rare disease called noma. Noma causes body tissue around the mouth and face to die. The children of the Roma camp commonly suffered from the disease. At one point, Mengele had two Roma children killed just so that he could examine their detached heads.

MENGELE'S EXPERIMENTS COME TO AN END

Our understanding of Mengele's nature comes from surviving prisoners who served on his medical team.

They remembered his ability to show civility and then within seconds commit a heinous or murderous act. Mengele purposefully scheduled gassings of Jewish prisoners on Jewish religious holidays. He sometimes wore a pistol, which was a strange thing for a doctor to wear.

Mengele's entire goal at Auschwitz was to uphold Nazi supremacy. Some people who knew Mengele personally believed that he did horrible things only because of the Nazi movement and his faithful belief in it. One friend even believed that if the war and Nazism had never happened, Mengele might have been a harmless but slightly cruel professor at a German university—a world away from the medical monster that he became at Auschwitz.

Toward the end of 1944, the German war effort was failing. Massive Allied invasions were underway. Some German officials plotted to assassinate Hitler, but their attempt failed. The Russian army was succeeding against Germany and had managed to liberate a German death camp. The Allies had liberated several cities that had been occupied by German armies. Prisoner and ghetto revolts had taken place, even at Auschwitz. The Auschwitz prison revolt resulted in the destruction of one of the crematoriums.

Mengele's experiments were also coming to an end. Prisoner trains to Auschwitz had already begun to slow by the middle of 1944. By the end of 1944, the death camp was being dismantled and plans to evacuate the camp were underway. However, the gassings and experiments continued until the last possible moment. The final roll call at the camp was performed on January 17, 1945. A massive evacuation began the next day, when thousands of prisoners were forced to march on foot toward Austria. Other prisoners were shot or crammed into train cars without a specific destination scheduled. Ten days after the final roll call, the Soviet armies liberated Auschwitz, freeing the last of the prisoners, who numbered nearly seven thousand.

Mengele left the camp on the same day as the final roll call. Days before leaving camp, Mengele collected all of his medical papers. He did not want them to fall into the hands of the enemy. He was assigned to another concentration camp, which he fled on February 18 to avoid the advancing Soviet troops. While fleeing, he joined a group of retreating German forces. Mengele switched his

SS uniform for one of theirs and tried to blend in among the soldiers. He met an old colleague who helped him stay with the group. Mengele gave his

On January 27, 2015, survivors of the atrocities at Auschwitz, including Mirosław Celka (shown above), visited the camp on the seventieth anniversary of its liberation. Shortly before the camp was liberated, Mengele collected his medical papers and escaped.

medical papers to a nurse he met while with the group. He believed that she would be able to hide the papers and, eventually, return them to him.

On April 30, 1945, Adolf Hitler committed suicide. Germany surrendered on May 8, 1945. On June 15, American forces captured more than ten thousand German soldiers in the same region where Mengele's group was. The group was captured a few days later. At this time, Mengele's name was listed as a principal war criminal and he was wanted for mass murder. During questioning, Mengele used his real name, but he was not identified as an SS member. He also lacked the tattoo with which all SS members were branded. It is believed that the American prisoner of war (POW) camp officials

After Germany surrendered, American forces rounded up German troops and kept them in POW camps, such as the one shown above. Mengele was briefly detained in a POW camp but managed to escape without being identified as the infamous doctor wanted for war crimes.

hadn't received the wanted list and therefore didn't identify him as the notorious SS doctor.

MENGELE ON THE RUN

While detained in the American POW camp, Mengele suffered from extreme depression. He was examined by a fellow prisoner who was a doctor as well. Mengele told the doctor how he feared being discovered. The doctor, Fritz Ulmann, had access to the office that released identification papers. Dr. Ulmann made a set of identification papers in his own name for Mengele to use so that he wouldn't get caught. Although there are conflicting reports as to when Mengele was set free, it definitely happened toward the end of 1945.

He was released in a Bavarian town close to Donauwörth, where a prewar school friend named Albert Miller lived and worked as a veterinarian. He decided to walk to the town. On the way, he was offered the use of a bike by a farmer who had an extra one. Along the way, Mengele hid his real identification papers in the empty handlebar of the bike. When he parted company with the farmer, he forgot about them. From that moment, he only had one set of papers, identifying him as Fritz Ulmann. The U.S. government later carried out an extensive search for the papers on many old bikes throughout Bavaria, but the papers were never found.

Because of his family's power, and the unwillingness of many Germans to believe what was being said about Nazi atrocities, many people helped Mengele evade capture. He relied on his friend Dr. Miller to relay messages to his family. He eventually fled from the Millers when he thought capture was near. He relied on another set of friends for his next lodging. They also helped him to find a safe place that was not associated with anyone he knew. He was sent to work on a farm, where he stayed until 1948. Ironically, one of his farm jobs was to select and separate good potatoes from bad potatoes.

While Mengele was in hiding, his friends and family hid the truth. His wife and family told authorities that Mengele was dead. Irene even visited Mengele while he was at the farm. Dr. von Verschuer destroyed all evidence of his correspondence with Mengele. Mengele even managed to get his medical papers back from the nurse he met while fleeing.

ESCAPE TO SOUTH AMERICA

In the spring of 1949, Mengele decided to leave the country in order to make a new life for himself. His wife refused to leave with him. Mengele was forced to flee alone. He made his way to Argentina by using his father's vast business connections. He arrived on

August 26, 1949. Mengele kept in touch with and visited his family over the years, but his marriage to Irene was finished. To his son, Rolf, he became known as Uncle Fritz. His true identity was only revealed to Rolf years later.

Disappearing into Argentina was not difficult for Mengele. He found Buenos Aires to be a wonderful place, as did many other ex-Nazis on the run. He even joined a group of prominent Argentine leaders and resettled Nazis. Mengele worked as a salesman, selling products from his father's foundry. He even remarried. His father arranged for him to marry Martha, the widow of Mengele's brother, Karl Jr. The elder Mengele arranged a meeting in the Swiss Alps for Josef, Martha, Martha's son, and Rolf. The meeting went well, and Martha and her son eventually moved to Argentina. Martha and Mengele were married in 1958, and Mengele used his real name to apply for the marriage license.

At one point, Mengele had problems with the Buenos Aires police, who suspected that he was practicing medicine without a license. What led them to this suspicion is unknown, and it frightened Mengele. Martha and her son remained in Buenos Aires, but Mengele decided to flee to Paraguay. A person could easily enter Paraguay without paperwork and disappear there, which is why Mengele chose it. Martha and her son made regular visits to his new home there.

Over the next several years, Mengele managed to stay free. Through the efforts of those who were

Josef Mengele, el
Médico Asesino
de Auschwitz

In the July 11, 1960, issue of *Correo de la tarde,* several artist sketches of Mengele's likeness are shown under the headline: "Wanted criminal has disappeared from his Buenos Aires home." To evade capture, Mengele fled Argentina and moved to Paraguay.

determined to see justice done, it became known that Mengele was alive and on the run in South America. Multiple governments failed in attempts to have Mengele captured. Those who visited him in his new life never disclosed his whereabouts. The Mengele family photo album has photos of Mengele well into his later years.

EVADING JUSTICE

Josef Mengele was charged with crimes against humanity, including selections, lethal phenol injections, beatings, shootings, and other forms of deliberate killing. He was never tried for those crimes. Whether he ever experienced true remorse for his hideous behavior will never be known. What is known is that Mengele was a product of his culture and times. Germany and its circumstances helped to shape the villainous man who came to be known as the Angel of Death. Instead of being hanged like his Nazi colleagues, Mengele spent the rest of his life on borrowed time.

It is believed that in February 1979, Mengele drowned in the waters off the coast of Bertioga, Brazil. Friends of Mengele brought his body back to the beach after seeing him struggle in the surf. His death was kept a secret by family and friends. The bones were finally exhumed by authorities in 1985, and in 1992 DNA testing declared them to be Josef Mengele's.

Eva Mozes Kor and other survivors of Auschwitz continue to share their testimony of the horrific crimes against humanity that they witnessed. Kor's *Surviving the Angel of Death* recounts the twin's interactions with Mengele, Auschwitz's Angel of Death.

In years since, new insights have shed light on Mengele's life in hiding. In 2007, the United States Holocaust Memorial Museum acquired the Höcker Album, a photograph album of Auschwitz staff with several previously unseen photographs of Mengele. In 2010 and 2011, more than thirty volumes of Mengele's diaries from Brazil were sold in an auction.

Today, the Mengele family foundry in Günzburg continues to run. In 2010, it was acquired by Lely, a Netherlands-based agricultural equipment manufacturer, but the Bavarian foundry still operates under the Mengele family name. There is even a street in the small town that bears Karl Mengele's name. Ironically, Josef—who set out to find fame on his own despite his family's success—is not memorialized in his birthplace. He is, instead, memorialized in the accounts of his victims and in history books. His legacy persists as one of modern history's most notorious villains.

TIMELINE

March 16, 1911 Josef Mengele is born in Günzburg, Germany.

1914–1918 Germany participates in World War I under the leadership of Kaiser Wilhelm II.

1919–1933 Following World War I, Germany has a democratic government during a period known as the Weimar Republic.

1925–1926 Hitler's autobiographical manifesto *Mein Kampf* is published over two volumes, detailing his political beliefs.

October 1930 Mengele begins his studies of medicine and philosophy at the University of Munich.

1931 Mengele joins the Stahlhelm, a youth group with nationalistic, anti-Semitic goals.

October 11, 1931 An alliance is formed between the Nazis, the Steel Helmets, and other nationalist groups.

August 2, 1934 President Paul von Hindenburg dies, leading Hitler to take power and proclaim himself Führer.

1935 Mengele earns a PhD in physical anthropology from the University of Munich.

September 15, 1935 Two anti-Semitic laws known as the Nuremberg Laws are enacted, stripping Jews and other non-Aryans of their German citizenship and preventing intermarriage between Aryans and Jews.

January 1937 Mengele begins work as a research assistant at the Institute for Hereditary Biology and Racial Hygiene in Frankfurt.

1937 Mengele joins the Nazi Party.

1938 Mengele publishes his medical dissertation and earns his medicine degree from the University of Frankfurt. He also joins the SS.

1938–1942 Mengele serves in the SS.

November 9–10, 1938 On a night known as Kristallnacht, thousands of Jewish businesses and synagogues are destroyed by SA troopers and unruly mobs.

July 28, 1939 Mengele marries Irene Schönbein.

September 1939 Germany invades Poland.

May 1940 Auschwitz opens.

June 1941 Germany invades the Soviet Union.

July 1941 The Final Solution begins.

May 1943 Mengele is stationed at Auschwitz.

June 1944 Allies mount a massive attack against Germany.

January 17, 1945 Mengele leaves Auschwitz, and his flight from justice begins.

January 27, 1945 The Soviet army liberates the Auschwitz concentration camp.

April 1945 Hitler commits suicide.

May 1945 Germany surrenders.

April 17, 1949 Mengele flees Germany for South America.

September 1956 Mengele obtains identity documents from both the local Buenos Aires police and the West Germany Embassy under his real name. A clerical oversight allows him to go unnoticed as the sought-after war criminal.

Summer 1958 Mengele marries his widowed sister-in-law, Martha, using his real name on the Argentine marriage certificate.

September 1958 After Argentine police investigate his medical practice, Mengele flees to Paraguay to further avoid capture.

Early 1961 Mengele leaves Paraguay for Brazil with the help of a former Nazi then living in Brazil.

February 7, 1979 Mengele drowns while swimming with friends in Bertioga, Brazil.

June 1985 The bones of a body in South America believed to be Mengele's are exhumed. Later DNA testing proves the bones are indeed Mengele's.

January 27, 2015 World leaders and Holocaust survivors gather to celebrate the 70th anniversary of the liberation of Auschwitz.

GLOSSARY

Allies Great Britain, the United States, the Soviet Union, and other nations that fought against Nazi Germany and its allies during World War II.

anti-Semitism Prejudice or discrimination against people of the Jewish religion.

Aryan The Nazis used this term to describe people of Northern European descent, usually with blond hair and blue eyes.

Aryanization The taking over of Jewish jobs and businesses by non-Jewish German people.

asocials People deemed unworthy by Nazis, such as Gypsies, homosexuals, and the mentally and physically disabled.

Auschwitz The largest Nazi concentration and death camp, located in Poland.

concentration camps Prison camps built to hold Jews, political prisoners, and asocials.

death camp Camp where mass numbers of people were killed.

Einsatzgruppen Mobile killing units of the SS.

eugenics A science that focuses on improving hereditary qualities of a race, usually by control of human mating.

Final Solution A plan for the complete destruction of European Jews.

Führer A German word meaning leader.

Lebensraum A Nazi term meaning living space.

Mischlinge A Nazi term for people of mixed German and Jewish ancestry.

Nazi An abbreviation for the National Socialist German Workers Party.

occupation When a country at war takes over an area of another country or territory.

propaganda The spreading of ideas, misinformation, and rumors for the purpose of helping a cause.

SA (Sturmabteilung) A Nazi military branch, also known as Storm Troopers or Brown Shirts.

Selektionen The Nazi system of separating prisoners and deciding who was to live and who was to die.

SS (Schutzstaffel) A large Nazi military group, also known as the Protection Squad.

Stahlhelm The Steel Helmets, a nationalistic, anti-Semitic group.

Third Reich The Nazi German Empire.

Weimar Republic The German government established after World War I, which governed from 1919–1933.

CANDLES Holocaust Museum and Education Center
1532 South Third Street
Terre Haute, IN 47802
(812) 234-7881
Website: http://www.candlesholocaustmuseum.org
Founded by Eva Mozes Kor, a survivor of Mengele's
inhumane human experimentation at Auschwitz,
CANDLES educates the public about the Holocaust with firsthand experiences of survivors.

Friends of Simon Wiesenthal Center for Holocaust
Studies (FSWC)
5075 Yonge Street
Toronto, ON M2N 6C6
Canada
(416) 864-9735
(866) 864-9735
Website: http://www.friendsofsimonwiesenthal
center.com
FSWC is a Canadian organization dedicated to
eradicating racism and anti-Semitism from the
world, while promoting government policies of
tolerance and equality for all citizens.

The Jewish Museum
1109 5th Avenue
New York, NY 10128

(212) 423-3200
Website: http://thejewishmuseum.org
The Jewish Museum is a hub for artists, students,
    and educators to contemplate Jewish art, life,
    and history through a number of exhibitions and
    educational talks.

Los Angeles Museum of the Holocaust (LAMOTH)
100 South The Grove Drive
Los Angeles, CA 90036
(323) 651-3704
Website: http://www.lamoth.org
LAMOTH has a mission based on the concepts
    of commemoration and education. As a primary
    source institution, it documents the Holocaust
    and provides free public educations on its
    atrocities.

Montreal Holocaust Memorial Centre
5151, Chemin de la Côte-Sainte-Catherine
(Cummings House)
Montreal, QC H3W 1M6
Canada
(514) 345-2605
Website: http://www.mhmc.ca/en
The Montreal Holocaust Memorial Centre serves
    as a place for memory and commemoration of
    victims of the Holocaust.

Museum of Tolerance
9786 West Pico Boulevard

Los Angeles, CA 90035
(310) 553-8403
Website: http://www.museumoftolerance.com
Since 1993, the Museum of Tolerance has been
    dedicated to promoting the principles of
    human rights, equality, and tolerance.

National WWII Museum
945 Magazine Street
New Orleans, LA 70130
(504) 528-1944
Website: http://www.nationalww2museum.org
Opened in 2000, the National WWII Museum features
    over 178,000 square feet of exhibits. It is a state-of-
    the-art educational institution dedicated to
    preserving the memory of one of the twentieth
    century's deadliest global conflicts.

Simon Wiesenthal Center
1399 South Roxbury Drive
Los Angeles, CA 90035
(310) 553-9036
(800) 900-9036
Website: http://www.wiesenthal.com
The Simon Wisenthal Center is a human rights
    organization committed to combatting anti-
    Semitism, hate, and intolerance around
    the world. In addition to its headquarters,
    branches operate in New York, Toronto, Miami,
    Chicago, Paris, Buenos Aires, and Jerusalem.

United States Holocaust Memorial Museum
(USHMM)
100 Raoul Wallenberg Place SW
Washington, DC 20024
(202) 488-0400
Website: http://www.ushmm.org
Since 1993, the USHMM serves to inspire visitors
and eternally memorialize the victims of one
of the twentieth century's darkest moments. It
works to promote tolerance and human rights
through education, exhibits, and interactive
programming.

WEBSITES

Because of the changing nature of Internet links,
Rosen Publishing has developed an online list of
websites related to the subject of this book. This site
is updated regularly. Please use this link to access
this list:

http://www.rosenlinks.com/HOLO/Meng

Brezina, Corona. *Nazi Architects of the Holocaust*. New York, NY: The Rosen Publishing Group, Inc., 2015.

Byers, Ann. *Auschwitz, Bergen-Belsen, Treblinka: The Holocaust Camps*. Berkeley Heights, NJ: Enslow Publishers, 2014.

Deem, James M. *Auschwitz: Voices from the Death Camp*. Berkeley Heights, NJ: Enslow Publishers, 2012.

Fitzgerald, Stephanie. *Children of the Holocaust*. Mankato, MN: Compass Point Books, 2011.

Frank, Anne. *The Diary of a Young Girl*. Abridged Ed. London, England: Puffin, 2015.

Kor, Eva Mozes Kor, and Lisa Rojany-Buccieri. *Surviving the Angel of Death: The Story of a Mengele Twin in Auschwitz*. Terre Haute, IN: Tanglewood, 2009.

Levin, Ira. *The Boys from Brazil: A Novel*. New York, NY: Random House, 1976.

Lifton, Robert Jay. *The Nazi Doctors: Medical Killing and the Psychology of Genocide*. New Ed. New York, NY: Basic Books, 2000.

Meyer, Susan. *Nazi Concentration Camps: A Policy of Genocide*. New York, NY: The Rosen Publishing Group, Inc., 2015.

Posner, Gerald L., and John Ware. *Mengele: The Complete Story*. New York: Cooper Square Press, 2006.

Sheehan, Sean. *Auschwitz* (A Place in History). Mankato, MN: Arcturus Publishing, 2010.

Steinacher, Gerald. *Nazis on the Run: How Hitler's Henchmen Fled Justice*. New York, NY: Oxford University Press, 2011.

Stille, Darlene R. *Architects of the Holocaust*. Mankato, MN: Compass Point Books, 2011.

Walters, Guy. *Hunting Evil: The Nazi War Criminals Who Escaped and the Quest to Bring Them to Justice*. New York, NY: Broadway Books, 2009.

INDEX

ABOUT THE AUTHOR

Jeremy Klar is a writer and history buff. He currently lives in Brooklyn, NY.

Henrietta M. Lily is a children's book author and illustrator from New York City. She majored in creative nonfiction writing in college.

PHOTO CREDITS

Cover, p. 52 Hulton Archive/Archive Photos/Getty Images; p. 5 Ryan Donnell/ Aurora//Getty Images; pp. 6-7 (background) Ingo JezierskiPhotographer's Choice/Getty Images; pp. 6-7 (inset), 24-25, 40, 45, 63 ullstein bild/Getty Images; pp. 11, 29, 47, 61, 78 Rolf E. Staerk/ Shutterstock.com; p. 12 dpa/ picturealliance/dpa/AP Images; pp. 15, 93 © TopFoto/The Image Works; pp. 16-17 © Scheri/Sueddeutsche Zeitung Photo/The Image Works; pp. 22-23 © Mary Evans Picture Library/The Image Works; p. 27 © Flirt/Alamy; pp. 30-31, 38-39 Hulton Archive/Getty Images; p. 33 Carl De Souza/AFP/Getty Images; p. 35 Keystone-France/Gamma-Keystone/Getty Images; pp. 42-43 © World History Archive/Alamy; p. 49 Fred Ramage/Hulton Archive/Getty Images; pp. 51, 71 Galerie Bilderwelt/Hulton Archive/Getty Images; p. 56 Roger Viollet/ Getty Images; pp. 58, 88-89 Popperfoto/Getty Images; pp. 64-65 Keystone/ Hulton Archive/Getty Images; pp. 68-69 David Clapp/Oxford Scientific/Getty Images; pp. 74-75 Universal Images Group/Getty Images; pp 80-81 © AP Images; pp. 86-87 Odd Andersen/AFP/Getty Images; p. 95 Janek Skarzynski/ AFP/Getty Images; interior pages background textures and graphics Aleksandr Bryliaev/Shutterstock.com, kak2s/Shutterstock.com, argus/Shutterstock.com, Sfio Cracho/Shutterstock.com; back cover Ventura/Shutterstock.com

Designer: Michael Moy; Editor: Jacob Steinberg;
Photo Researcher: Rona Tuccillo